MIKAELA SHIFFRIN

The Girl Who Conquered the Snow-
Biography For Kids

Bruce L. Jimenez

Copyright @ 2024 By Bruce L. Jimenez

All rights reserved. No part of this book may be reproduced, distributed, or transmitted in any form or by any means, including photocopying, recording, or other electronic or mechanical methods, without the prior written permission of the publisher, except in the case of brief quotations embodied in critical reviews and specific other noncommercial uses permitted by copyright law.

TABLE OF CONTENTS

INTRODUCTION: MEET MIKAELA SHIFFRIN

CHAPTER 1: A SNOWY START

CHAPTER 2: GROWING UP ON THE SLOPES

CHAPTER 3: BIG DREAMS AND HARD WORK

CHAPTER 4: OVERCOMING CHALLENGES

CHAPTER 5: RISING STAR

CHAPTER 6: ACHIEVEMENTS

CHAPTER 7: GIVING BACK

CHAPTER 8: HOBBIES AND INTERESTS

CHAPTER 9: FANBASE

CHAPTER 10: IMPACT

CHAPTER 11: FUN FACTS ABOUT MIKAELA SHIFFRIN
CONCLUSION: INSPIRATION TO ALL
QUIZ: HOW MUCH DO YOU KNOW ABOUT MIKAELA SHIFFRIN

INTRODUCTION: MEET MIKAELA SHIFFRIN

Hi there! Are you ready to meet an amazing skier? Her name is Mikaela Shiffrin, and she is one of the best skiers in the world. Mikaela is known for her incredible speed and skill on the snow. But her story is not just about racing down mountains; it's also about hard work, dedication, and following your dreams.

Mikaela was born on March 13, 1995, in a small town called Vail, Colorado. Vail is famous for its beautiful ski slopes and snowy mountains. Mikaela's parents, Jeff and Eileen Shiffrin, loved skiing, and they introduced Mikaela to the sport when she was just a little girl. They took her to the mountains to ski, and that's where Mikaela discovered her love for the sport.

From the very beginning, Mikaela was a natural on skis. She practiced a lot, and with each passing year, she got better and better. She started competing in ski races when she was very young. Her hard work paid off, and she began winning races and earning medals.

When she was a teenager, Mikaela became a star. She won her first World Cup race at just 17 years old! This was a huge achievement because the World Cup is a big series of races where the best skiers from around the world compete. Winning a race at such a young age showed everyone that Mikaela was very special.

Mikaela's skiing style is amazing. She zooms down the slopes with incredible speed and precision. She is known for her quick turns and smooth moves, which make her one of the fastest and most skilled skiers. Her talent has earned her many awards, including gold medals in the Winter Olympics, which is a big competition where countries from all over the world come together to compete.

But Mikaela is not just a fantastic skier; she is also a kind and inspiring person. She always encourages others to work hard and never give up on their dreams. Mikaela's story teaches us that with determination and passion, we can achieve great things.

So, get ready to learn more about Mikaela Shiffrin's exciting adventures on the slopes and how she became a skiing superstar. Her journey is full of challenges, triumphs, and lots of fun. Are you excited to step into her world? Let's go.

CHAPTER 1: A SNOWY START

Imagine a place where the ground is covered with a soft, white blanket of snow. This is the world where Mikaela Shiffrin began her amazing journey. It all started in a snowy town called Vail, Colorado. Vail is known for its stunning mountains and fantastic ski slopes, perfect for someone who loves skiing like Mikaela did.

Mikaela was born on March 13, 1995, in this snowy wonderland. From the moment she was little, she was surrounded by snow. Her parents, Jeff and Eileen Shiffrin, loved skiing, and they couldn't wait to share their passion with Mikaela. They took her to the slopes when she was just a baby, and by the time she was three years old, she was already trying to ski on her own!

When Mikaela was a little girl, she spent a lot of time at the ski resort with her family. They had so much fun together, sliding down the hills and making snow angels. Mikaela loved the thrill of skiing, and she was always excited to go faster and learn new things. She practiced a lot and was determined to get better each day.

One of Mikaela's earliest memories is of racing her parents down the hills. Even though she was young, she had a natural talent for skiing. She was quick and agile, zooming down the slopes with a big smile on her face. Her parents saw her potential and encouraged her to keep practicing.

As Mikaela grew older, she began to compete in local ski races. She was nervous at first, but she was also excited to show what she could do. The races were challenging, but Mikaela never gave up. She worked hard to improve her skills, and her dedication started to pay off. She began winning races and earning medals, which made her even more excited to ski.

Mikaela's snowy start was just the beginning of her incredible journey. She learned that with hard work and determination, she could achieve amazing things. Her story shows us that even the smallest start can lead to big dreams and fantastic achievements.

So remember, just like Mikaela, if you have a dream or something you enjoy, don't be afraid to work hard and practice. Whether it's skiing, drawing, or playing a sport, every little bit of effort helps you get closer to your goals. Keep going, and you might just reach your amazing heights!

Believe in yourself, keep practicing, and never stop dreaming. You never know where your snowy start might lead you.

CHAPTER 2: GROWING UP ON THE SLOPES

Growing up in Vail, Colorado, Mikaela Shiffrin's childhood was like a magical adventure in a winter wonderland. The snow-covered mountains were her playground, and skiing was more than just a sport—it was a way of life.

From a very young age, Mikaela spent almost every day on the slopes with her family. Her parents, Jeff and Eileen Shiffrin, loved skiing and made sure Mikaela had plenty of chances to practice. They would go up to the mountains together, enjoying the crisp, fresh air and the beautiful snowy scenery. Mikaela's excitement was contagious, and she quickly became a skilled skier.

As she grew older, Mikaela's skills on the slopes continued to improve. She joined a local ski team where she learned from experienced coaches and trained with other young skiers. Training was hard work, but Mikaela enjoyed every moment. She practiced skiing through gates, making quick turns, and speeding down the slopes. Each day, she challenged herself to become better and faster.

Mikaela's family supported her every step of the way. They cheered her on during races and celebrated her achievements, big and small. Her parents taught her the importance of being dedicated and working hard, but they also made sure to have fun. Whether it was building snow forts or having snowball fights, Mikaela's childhood was filled with joy and laughter.

Despite the fun, Mikaela faced challenges too. Skiing at a high level can be tough and requires a lot of practice. Sometimes, she would fall or not do as well as she hoped in a race. But Mikaela didn't let these setbacks stop her. She learned from her mistakes, practiced even more, and came back stronger each time.

Growing up on the slopes taught Mikaela many important lessons. She learned that hard work and perseverance are key to achieving her goals. She also discovered that even when things don't go as planned, it's important to keep trying and stay positive.

So, if you have something you love to do, remember Mikaela's story. Whether it's skiing, dancing, or playing an instrument, don't be afraid to put in the effort and practice. You might face challenges along the way, but with determination and a positive attitude, you can overcome them and achieve your dreams.

Keep working hard, believe in yourself, and enjoy the journey. Just like Mikaela, you can turn your passions into amazing achievements and have fun along the way.

CHAPTER 3: BIG DREAMS AND HARD WORK

Mikaela Shiffrin's journey from a young skier on the slopes of Vail to becoming one of the world's top ski racers is a great example of how big dreams and hard work can lead to amazing achievements.

As Mikaela grew older, she started setting bigger goals for herself. She dreamed of becoming a champion skier and competing in major races all over the world. But having big dreams is just the beginning. To make those dreams come true, Mikaela knew she had to work very hard.

Training for skiing is not easy. Mikaela spent hours each day practicing her skills. She would wake up early, put on her ski gear, and head to the slopes. Even when it was cold and snowy, she would train. She practiced skiing through gates, making sharp turns, and speeding down the hills. Her coaches helped her improve, giving her tips on how to be faster and more precise.

Mikaela also had to stay fit and strong. She did exercises to build her strength and agility. Skiing requires strong muscles and quick reflexes, so she worked on running, lifting weights, and doing exercises that helped her stay in top shape. It wasn't always fun, but Mikaela knew that it was important to be in great condition to perform well in races.

Sometimes, things didn't go as planned. Mikaela would face challenges, like tough competition or a race that didn't go well. But instead of getting discouraged, she used these moments as opportunities to learn and grow. She practiced even harder, making adjustments and improving her techniques. Her dedication paid off when she began winning races and earning medals.

One of Mikaela's biggest achievements came when she won her first World Cup race at just 17 years old. The World Cup is a big competition where the best skiers from around the world come together to race. Winning a World Cup race showed that all of Mikaela's hard work was paying off and that she was one of the best skiers in the world.

Mikaela's story teaches us that big dreams can come true if we are willing to put in the effort. So, if you have a dream, whether it's in sports, art, or anything else you love, remember that hard work is key. Keep practicing, stay focused, and believe in yourself. Just like Mikaela Shiffrin, you can reach your goals and make your dreams come true.

Keep dreaming big and working hard—you're capable of amazing things.

CHAPTER 4: OVERCOMING CHALLENGES

Every champion faces challenges along their journey, and Mikaela Shiffrin is no exception. Her path to becoming one of the world's best skiers was filled with obstacles, but she showed us that overcoming challenges is an important part of achieving greatness.

When Mikaela was starting, she faced many difficulties. Skiing at a high level is not just about being fast; it's about handling tough conditions, learning new techniques, and staying mentally strong. Mikaela practiced tirelessly, but there were times when things didn't go as planned.

One of the biggest challenges Mikaela faced was dealing with injuries. Skiing is an intense sport that can put a lot of strain on the body. Mikaela had to take time off to recover from injuries, which was frustrating and disheartening. But instead of letting these setbacks stop her, she used them as opportunities to get stronger. She worked with her coaches and doctors to heal properly and come back even better.

Another challenge was handling the pressure of competition. As Mikaela's success grew, so did the expectations. People began to expect her to win every race, and this pressure could be overwhelming. But Mikaela learned how to stay focused and not let the pressure affect her performance. She practiced staying calm and confident, which helped her perform her best even under stress.

Mikaela also faced tough competition from other talented skiers. Sometimes she didn't win, and that could be disappointing. However, she used these experiences to learn and improve. She studied her races, worked on her weaknesses, and came back stronger. Mikaela's ability to learn from every race, whether she won or not, was key to her success.

Despite these challenges, Mikaela never gave up. She kept working hard, believing in herself, and pushing through difficulties. Her story shows that overcoming challenges is a part of the journey to success. It's not always easy, but facing obstacles and finding ways to overcome them makes you stronger and more resilient.

If you're facing challenges in your own life, remember Mikaela Shiffrin's story. Whether it's a tough subject at school, a sport you're trying to master, or a personal goal you're working towards, don't be discouraged. Keep pushing forward, stay positive, and use challenges as chances to learn and grow.

Believe in yourself and know that you can overcome any obstacle that comes your way. Just like Mikaela, you have the strength and determination to reach your goals and achieve your dreams.

CHAPTER 5: RISING STAR

Mikaela Shiffrin's journey to becoming a skiing superstar is a story of talent, hard work, and rising above challenges. From a young skier on the slopes of Vail to a global champion, Mikaela's rise to stardom is truly inspiring.

As Mikaela continued to compete in ski races, her talent and dedication began to shine brightly. She was not just another skier; she was a rising star with incredible potential. Her speed, precision, and determination caught the attention of many. People started to notice that she was not only skilled but also had a special spark that set her apart.

Mikaela's breakthrough moment came when she won her first World Cup race at just 17 years old. The World Cup is a series of races where the best skiers from all over the world compete. Winning at such a young age was a huge achievement and marked the beginning of Mikaela's rise to the top of the skiing world. It was a sign that she was not just a rising star but a future legend in the making.

With each race, Mikaela's reputation grew. She continued to win races and earn medals, proving that her first victory was just the beginning. She became known for her incredible technique, her ability to handle tough conditions, and her fierce determination. Mikaela's performances on the slopes made headlines, and she quickly became a favorite among fans and fellow skiers alike.

As a rising star, Mikaela faced new challenges and responsibilities. People expected her to perform at her best in every race, and she had to learn how to manage this pressure. She worked closely with her coaches and team to stay focused and keep improving. Mikaela's ability to handle the expectations and continue performing at a high level showed her strength and character.

Mikaela's rise to stardom was not just about her skills on the slopes. It was also about her positive attitude and dedication to the sport. She became a role model for young skiers, showing them that with hard work and perseverance, they could achieve their dreams too.

So, if you have a dream and are working hard to achieve it, remember Mikaela Shiffrin's story.

Just like Mikaela, you have the potential to shine and become a star in your way. Keep believing in yourself, work hard, and stay focused on your goals. Your rise to greatness could be just around the corner!

Believe in your dreams, keep working hard, and know that you have the power to become a rising star in whatever you choose to do. The sky is the limit.

CHAPTER 6: ACHIEVEMENTS

An achievement is something you accomplish through hard work, effort, and dedication. It's a success or a milestone that shows you've reached a goal or made significant progress in something you care about. Achievements can be big or small, and they are a way of recognizing your hard work and talents.

Now, let's take a look at some of Mikaela Shiffrin's amazing achievements, both from earlier in her career and the newest ones that show just how talented and hardworking she is.

When Mikaela was just 17 years old, she won her first World Cup race in Austria. This was a huge achievement because it meant she was one of the fastest skiers in the world, even at such a young age. She also became the youngest female skier to win a World Cup slalom title, showing that she was a rising star in the skiing world. At the Sochi Winter Olympics, Mikaela won her first Olympic medal, a silver, in the slalom event. This was an exciting moment and a big step in her career.

Mikaela has achieved even more incredible milestones. In 2021, she won the World Cup overall title, which is awarded to the best skier across all disciplines for the season. This achievement showed she was not only a top skier in one event but the best across multiple events. At the Beijing Winter Olympics in 2022, she won a gold medal in the giant slalom. This was a fantastic accomplishment and highlighted her skills on the world stage. Mikaela also set a new record in 2023 for the most World Cup race victories by any skier, male or female. This incredible achievement showed her dominance in the sport and her consistency over the years.

Mikaela Shiffrin's achievements are a testament to her hard work, determination, and love for skiing. Each milestone represents a goal she has reached and a new height she has achieved in her career. Her story teaches us that with dedication and effort, we can achieve great things and make our dreams come true. Keep working hard, stay focused, and celebrate your successes along the way. You have the potential to achieve amazing things, just like Mikaela Shiffrin.

CHAPTER 7: GIVING BACK

Giving back is a special way of helping others and making a positive difference in the world. For Mikaela Shiffrin, giving back is an important part of her life and career. She understands that while achieving personal success is wonderful, it's also important to use that success to help others.

Mikaela is involved in various charitable activities and community efforts. One of her key initiatives is supporting young athletes. She often participates in events that raise funds to help kids who want to get involved in sports but might not have the resources to do so. By doing this, she helps make sports accessible to more children, giving them opportunities to follow their dreams just like she did.

She also supports organizations that focus on education and providing resources to children in need. Mikaela believes in the power of education and wants to ensure that every child has the chance to learn and grow. Her contributions help provide necessary supplies and support for schools and educational programs.

Mikaela is known for her involvement in environmental causes. She understands the importance of taking care of the planet and often participates in activities that promote sustainability and protect natural environments. By supporting these causes, she helps ensure that beautiful places like the mountains she loves remain healthy and enjoyable for future generations.

Mikaela Shiffrin's dedication to giving back shows us that success is not just about personal achievements but also about making a positive impact on the world. Her actions remind us that we can all contribute to our communities and help others, no matter how big or small our efforts may be.

If you have a passion or a talent, think about how you can use it to help others. Whether it's through volunteering, supporting a cause you care about, or simply being kind, you have the power to make a difference. Just like Mikaela, you can turn your successes into opportunities to give back and make the world a better place.

Remember, every small act of kindness and support can have a big impact. Keep finding ways to help others and use your talents to make a positive difference. You can create change and inspire others, just like Mikaela Shiffrin.

CHAPTER 8: HOBBIES AND INTERESTS

Mikaela Shiffrin's life is not just about skiing; she has a variety of hobbies and interests that keep her busy and happy outside of her intense training and competitions.

One of Mikaela's favorite pastimes is reading. She has a deep love for books and enjoys exploring different genres, from thrilling adventures and magical fantasy to insightful biographies and inspiring stories. Reading is not only a way for Mikaela to relax but also a means for her to learn new things and expand her imagination. It's a hobby that helps her unwind after a long day on the slopes and keeps her mind sharp.

Another significant part of Mikaela's life is her love for the outdoors. She enjoys hiking and exploring nature whenever she can. Hiking allows her to experience the beauty of the natural world and provides a peaceful escape from her busy skiing schedule. Being surrounded by mountains and forests helps her feel connected to nature and recharges her energy. It's also a great way for her to stay fit and enjoy time away from the competitive environment.

Mikaela also has a passion for photography. She finds joy in capturing moments and scenes through her camera lens. Photography allows her to see the world from different perspectives and appreciate its beauty in unique ways. Whether she's taking pictures of stunning landscapes or special moments with friends and family, photography is a creative outlet for Mikaela and a way for her to share her experiences with others.

Family and friends play an essential role in Mikaela's life as well. She cherishes the time she spends with them, whether it's cooking a meal together, playing games, or simply enjoying each other's company. These moments provide her with a sense of balance and happiness outside of her professional skiing career.

Mikaela Shiffrin's hobbies and interests highlight the importance of having activities you enjoy beyond your main focus. They help create a well-rounded and fulfilling life, offering relaxation, creativity, and joy. Engaging in different activities can also help you stay balanced and inspired, providing a break from intense work or training.

If you have hobbies or interests, it's important to make time for them. Whether it's reading, drawing, playing a sport, or any other activity you love, these hobbies are valuable for your happiness and well-being. They help you relax, express yourself, and connect with others.

Remember, exploring and nurturing your interests can bring a lot of joy and fulfillment into your life. So, keep enjoying the things that make you happy, and allow yourself to explore new passions and activities. Just like Mikaela Shiffrin, you have the power to find balance and joy through your hobbies and interests.

CHAPTER 9: FANBASE

A fanbase is a group of people who support, admire, and follow someone or something with great enthusiasm. Fans share a strong connection with their favorite celebrities, athletes, musicians, or other public figures. They enjoy celebrating their achievements, staying updated on their activities, and sometimes even participating in fan events or communities. Having a fanbase means having a group of dedicated supporters who are excited about what you do and are eager to share in your successes.

Mikaela Shiffrin has built an impressive fanbase over the years. Her fans come from all corners of the globe and share a deep admiration for her skiing skills and her vibrant personality. They are drawn to her incredible talent on the slopes, her dedication to her sport, and her positive attitude both on and off the snow.

Mikaela's fans express their support in many ways. They cheer her on during races, follow her updates on social media, and celebrate her victories with great enthusiasm. Her fanbase often wears Mikaela-themed clothing, waves flags, and participates in fan clubs or online forums where they discuss her achievements and share their excitement. The support from her fans is a big part of what makes her feel motivated and appreciated.

Mikaela also makes a point of connecting with her fans. She actively engages with them on social media platforms, sharing behind-the-scenes looks at her training, her travels, and her daily life. These interactions help her fans feel a personal connection and provide them with a glimpse into the life of their favorite skier. Mikaela also participates in fan events, autograph signings, and other activities where she takes the time to meet her supporters in person. These moments of personal connection are very special to both Mikaela and her fans.

Her fanbase plays a crucial role in her career. The encouragement and enthusiasm of her supporters provide her with an extra boost during tough training sessions and high-stakes competitions. Knowing that so many people believe in her and are cheering her on helps Mikaela stay focused and motivated.

Just like Mikaela, everyone can have their fanbase, whether it's friends, family, or people who appreciate their talents and efforts. If you have something you're passionate about, remember that there are people who will support and cheer you on. Building and nurturing your fanbase can be a source of motivation and joy, helping you to keep pursuing your dreams and sharing your achievements with others.

Whether you're an athlete, an artist, or following any other passion, cherish and appreciate the support of those who follow and admire you. Their encouragement can make a big difference in your journey, just as Mikaela Shiffrin's fanbase does for her. Every bit of support you receive is a reminder that you are making a positive impact and that there are people excited to see you succeed.

CHAPTER 10: IMPACT

Mikaela Shiffrin has had a profound impact on many aspects of life, not only through her impressive skiing achievements but also through her positive influence and community involvement. Her story and actions serve as an inspiration to people of all ages and backgrounds.

One of the most significant ways Mikaela has made an impact is by setting an exceptional example of dedication and perseverance. From a young age, she faced numerous challenges on her path to becoming a world-class skier. Her journey demonstrates that with hard work, determination, and a positive mindset, it is possible to overcome obstacles and achieve one's goals. Mikaela's story encourages others to pursue their dreams with the same level of commitment and resilience, showing that success is within reach with effort and perseverance.

Mikaela's impact on the skiing community is also noteworthy. Her remarkable performances and numerous victories have brought a heightened level of attention to the sport of skiing. By achieving such success on the global stage, she has inspired many young skiers to take up the sport and strive for excellence. Her achievements have contributed to the growth and popularity of skiing, helping to develop the sport at grassroots levels and encouraging more young people to get involved.

Mikaela is known for her charitable work and community involvement. She actively supports various causes, including initiatives that help young athletes, promote education, and protect the environment. Through her charitable efforts, Mikaela helps make a positive difference in the lives of others. Her support for youth sports programs ensures that more children have the opportunity to engage in athletics and develop their talents. Her contributions to educational causes help provide resources and opportunities for learning, while her environmental advocacy promotes the importance of taking care of our planet.

Mikaela Shiffrin's impact extends beyond her professional achievements and charitable work. She serves as a role model for handling success with humility and grace. Her ability to balance her incredible career with a commitment to giving back and staying grounded is a powerful example of how to lead with both talent and compassion. She demonstrates that being successful is not just about personal accomplishments but also about using one's influence to positively impact others.

Her influence reaches into everyday life as well. Mikaela's story teaches valuable lessons about chasing your passions, dealing with challenges, and supporting those around you. Her example shows that even amidst great success, it is important to remain focused on personal values and contribute to the community.

So, if you have a dream or a goal, remember the impact you can make by staying dedicated, helping others, and staying true to your values.

Just like Mikaela Shiffrin, you have the power to inspire those around you and create positive change in the world. Every action you take, no matter how small, can contribute to making a difference and achieving your dreams. By following Mikaela's example, you can work towards your goals while also making the world a better place.

CHAPTER 11: FUN FACTS ABOUT MIKAELA SHIFFRIN

Mikaela Shiffrin is an amazing skier who has achieved incredible things from a young age. She started skiing when she was just a toddler and has since become one of the fastest and most skilled skiers in the world. Here are some fun facts about Mikaela that show just how extraordinary she is:

1. Young Champion: Mikaela started skiing when she was only 2 years old! Even though she was small, she loved speeding down the slopes.

2. First Medal at 18: Mikaela won her first Olympic gold medal at just 18 years old! This showed everyone how talented she was.

3. A Love for Animals: Mikaela has a pet dog named "Ski" and she loves animals. Ski is often with her when she's not training or racing.

4. Super Fast on the Slopes: Mikaela is one of the fastest skiers in the world. She can ski down a mountain at speeds over 70 miles per hour!

5. Skiing Family: Her parents both love skiing too. Her mom was a ski racer, and her dad enjoyed skiing as a hobby. They taught her how to ski and helped her become great at it.

6. Favorite Foods: Mikaela loves to eat pasta and pizza. They give her lots of energy for her races!

7. A Big Fan of Books: Mikaela enjoys reading books, especially when she is traveling. She likes to learn new things and relax with a good story.

8. Smart in School: Mikaela is not just good at skiing; she is also a great student. She worked hard in school and kept up with her studies even when she was traveling.

9. Helping Others: Mikaela likes to help other people. She supports different charities and often talks about the importance of giving back to the community.

10. A Special Nickname: People call her "Mika," which is short for her full name, Mikaela. It's a friendly and easy name that fans and friends use to show how much they like her.

CONCLUSION: INSPIRATION TO ALL

Mikaela Shiffrin's journey from a young child learning to ski to becoming one of the world's top skiers is nothing short of extraordinary. Her story is a powerful testament to how passion, dedication, and relentless hard work can transform dreams into reality. Mikaela didn't achieve her success overnight; it took years of practice, perseverance, and pushing through challenges. Every victory she earned on the slopes came from countless hours of training, learning from her mistakes, and striving to be the best she could be.

Mikaela's achievements teach us an invaluable lesson: no matter how big or small our dreams may seem, they are within our reach if we believe in ourselves and put in the effort. Her story is a shining example that with determination and a positive attitude, we can overcome obstacles and achieve our goals. Whether you're aiming for success in sports, school, or any other area of life, Mikaela's journey shows us that staying focused and never giving up is essential to reaching our aspirations.

But Mikaela's impact extends far beyond her impressive medals and victories. Her generosity, kindness, and love for her family and pets highlight the importance of remaining true to oneself and making a positive difference in the world. Mikaela's dedication to helping others and supporting charitable causes reminds us that true success is not just about personal achievements but also about contributing to the well-being of those around us.

As you pursue your dreams and work towards your goals, let Mikaela Shiffrin's story be your inspiration. Embrace her example of unwavering determination, kindness, and resilience. Remember that challenges are growth opportunities and that every step forward brings you closer to your dreams. Believe in yourself, stay committed, and keep pushing forward, just like Mikaela. You have the power to make your dreams come true and, in doing so, inspire others to do the same. Your journey, like Mikaela's, can be a beacon of hope and motivation for everyone around you.

QUIZ: HOW MUCH DO YOU KNOW ABOUT MIKAELA SHIFFRIN

Test your knowledge about the amazing skier, Mikaela Shiffrin! Answer these fun questions to see how much you know about her.

1. How old was Mikaela when she started skiing?
   - A) 1 year old
   - B) 2 years old
   - C) 3 years old

2. What type of medal did Mikaela win at her first Olympics?
   - A) Silver
   - B) Gold

- C) Bronze

3. What is the name of Mikaela's pet dog?
   - A) Snow
   - B) Ski
   - C) Flake

4. How fast can Mikaela ski down a mountain?
   - A) 30 miles per hour
   - B) 50 miles per hour
   - C) 70 miles per hour

5. What kind of food does Mikaela love to eat?
   - A) Ice cream and cookies
   - B) Pasta and pizza
   - C) Hamburgers and fries

6. What did Mikaela's parents do that was similar to her hobby?

- A) They were both great swimmers
- B) They were both skiers
- C) They were both runners

7. What does Mikaela like to do when she is traveling?
   - A) Watch movies
   - B) Read books
   - C) Play video games

8. What is Mikaela's nickname?
   - A) Mike
   - B) Mika
   - C) Miki

9. Why is Mikaela's story inspiring?
   - A) Because she is good at math
   - B) Because she helps others and works hard
   - C) Because she likes to cook

10. What can we learn from Mikaela Shiffrin's story?

- A) To always stay indoors
- B) To believe in ourselves and never give up
- C) To avoid doing sports

ANSWERS

1. B) 2 years old
2. B) Gold
3. B) Ski
4. C) 70 miles per hour
5. B) Pasta and pizza
6. B) They were both skiers
7. B) Read books
8. B) Mika
9. B) Because she helps others and works hard
10. B) To believe in ourselves and never give up

No matter what your dreams are, remember Mikaela Shiffrin's story. She shows us that with hard work, determination, and kindness, we can achieve great things. Keep working towards your goals and believe in yourself—you can do amazing things too.

Made in the USA
Thornton, CO
01/22/25 21:22:32

4e89b8d9-0e5c-4232-9322-83ce9887ee26R01